MA. ..v1

Healing Poems

To all who are letting go of something or someone.

Live today. Let go of your attachment to your past as an excuse for your life conditions today. You are the product of the choices you are making right now.

- Dr. Wayne Dyer

Contents

Preface   iv

Look straight into the present   1

A bolt through the night   3

The stuff of life   5

A Light   7

Be focused on now   8

Breaking free   10

Close the book   11

Darkness   13

Dear Holy Spirit   15

One thought is true   17

Each day I will be reborn anew   19

Everyday is new   20

Freedom   22

Gather and Nourish relationships   23

Gonna Break Away   25

Hidden pain and healing rain   27

How do you heal the world   29

How high can you fly   31

I open the self   33

I will   35

Don't forget the present moment   37

Spread your love and light   39

Time to move on   40

It just takes one 42

It is time 44

Look straight into the present 46

New Beginnings 47

No matter 49

Nothing can hurt me 51

One thought can change your world 53

Our past and letting go 55

Outside and inside 57

Are you ready 59

I let go 61

Sail on 63

Seek and find 65

The flower 67

The flute of forgiveness 69

The Healing rain 70

The hole in my heart 72

The Little voice 74

the Looking glass 76

The Power is you 77

The precious present 78

The spirit I am 80

Be Kind 82

To tinker or tickle 83

Today is my day of release 84

Let it go 86

I'm at peace with the world 88

The change 89

The Quiet Center 91

Know or no 93

Within the Ocean of Love 95

What are those thoughts 98

What is the problem 100

You are invulnerable 102

Your worth 104

Straight into the present 105

Live in the now 107

Rest if you may 108

When the world gets you down 109

Thoughts on comparing and judging 111

One thought 112

Believe you can 113

About the Author 115

Also by Mark Helm 116

Preface

Healing - Poems about letting go and being in the present are about finding your peace of mind and helping you move through times when you need to let go of something, rather fears, relationships, self esteem, depression, anxiety, limits we place on ourselves or not feeling good enough or worthy. Being in the present becomes very healing in our life as we learn to let go of anything causing us pain and we understand keeping that thought within no longer serves our purpose to bring us happiness and joy.

You realize you have the power to let it go and make another choice.

I have added a few quotes at the bottom on some poems from other people and books. You will find some from A Course in Miracles which will have the abbreviation of ACIM and the link to the online version on the Foundation of Inner Peace web site - https://acim.org

A Light

Should I let the ray of light in?
Is it the right time for it to begin?
Or should I turn to let it pass
Draw the shade, for it won't last?

Searching my soul, it is hard to find
A deeper meaning to this light of mine.
If only a clue, a hint, to see
The soul, the mind, of what will be

What is to be, what shall come
What is the question, thy will be done.
I search my soul, I search my mind,
I search my heart, for all that is kind.

The light still shines, as does mine
But will it find a home, forever in time
To share a life with, to give life to.
This light shines brightly, making one with you

Nothing can dim the light that shines from within.
–Maya Angelou

Be focused on now

So many plans we make
so many moments we take
focused on what the future should be
keeping the past tight for all to see

So my friend be kind just for this moment
For within it, is all of Heaven's glory and light
within this moment is the only time their really is
and it shares with you in all its power and might

Being is staying within
Releasing any fears, guilt, or sins
Being is now and all there is
Now, God, Us, Her and His

Go boldly into the moment you share
with all, your brothers and sisters, and eternity
Peace, Joy, Light, and Love resides here
as the carpet rolls up, time's purpose becomes clear

Live in the present, launch yourself on every wave, find eternity in each moment.

– Henry David Thoreau

Breaking free

Breaking free from all those years
breaking free from falling tears
Leaving behind that which did not find
Letting go from a troubled mind

Crossing that bridge to another side
as the sea rolls away, with another tide
Moving beyond that deep emerald blue
washing away all that isn't true

And I break free, from a world which made
of things and time of yesterday
of thoughts and dreams which did not last
Yes I break free from that past

and moving on past stars and sky
moving upward, ever so high
the peace I have, the joy I share
breaking free I found, that love, is always there

Light cannot enter darkness when a mind believes in darkness, and
will not let it go. (ACIM, T-14.VII.5:1)

Close the book

There is a new chapter to be made
A new book to create and explore
One to enjoy as the pages are read
We can close the old and put it away

Life is a series of many books
the stories unfold in our lives
We make the forms
which become our norm

You know this well
Especially from relationships
They appear within a worldly dream
and the chapter ends but
you keep open the book

And you wish to read it again and again
for another chapter, another way for
the tale to end
for the prince and the princess to ride away
in some dreamland so far away

And you wonder why you don't turn the page
and place it on the shelf and move on oh wise sage
and perhaps somewhere inside you want to feel this way
but you don't understand that today

We all have those stories to be told and which have been
The Relationships, the hurts, and even the joys of life
should all be let go one by one
and place the book on the shelf
and move on in time

Forgive the past and let it go, for it is gone. ²You stand no longer on the ground that lies between the worlds. ³You have gone on, and reached the world that lies at Heaven's gate. (ACIM, T-26.V.14:1-3)

Darkness

Lights are out, night has drawn
the curtains closed, there is no dawn
a mind wonders and sinks into an abyss
seeking a sign, lights kiss

but it is not to be found
as we spiral on down
places some call hell
for there is no joy or comfort to tell

thoughts slip away, of brighter and more beautiful days
and darkness descends from a deepening haze
time matters not except for one thing
make it go away, a heart wishes to sing

a search for joy hidden under blankets by day
a search for meaning, what does God have to say
this is a place when pain is the sound
this is the place darkness is found

But know within you have the power
to move through the thunder and rain showers

Beyond the clouds the light can be found
You hold all within where your love abounds

Close your eyes, and hold his hand
and move through the veil and understand
Love goes with you sharing your light for all
and you are a beacon shining on this little blue ball
You are Love

Love holds no grievances. [9]When I let all my grievances go I will know I am perfectly safe. (ACIM, W-68.6:8-9)

Dear Holy Spirit

Lead the way for today
Let thoughts in the past slip away
Let thy light shine in time
Let love extend to all of thine

Lead me please for lost I seem
wondering on in a land of dreams
through a worldly maze
a cloudy haze

Help me understand
all is one
an endless song
and behind each form
each thought I seek
to find the path
the light, the meek

Let fear gently drift by
replaced by forgiveness

joy, laughter,
and loving minds

Let me see Love in all
as we travel on, this little ball

Your past is what you have taught yourself. [7]Let it all go. [8]Do not
attempt to understand any event or anything or anyone in its
"light," for the darkness in which you try to see can only obscure.
ACIM, T-14.XI.3:6-8)

One thought is true

We often times do
paint a not so colorful hue
thinking of our lives past
and making that memory last

Let those thoughts go!
That love does not show
Give them all away
For they do not show your way

The true thought of you
Shows joy and love always true
and any other thought we make real
covers up your glorious zeal

So when you find yourself
thinking to many bad thoughts
and crowding out the Light
don't despair, let go, to that which is bright

You have a gift to shine anything away
You have the power to let love shine today

You make the choice to be what you are always to be
You are the one to remember the love for you and me

Remember to pass by those clouds
for there beyond is your truth ever so bright

The shadow is the greatest teacher for how to come to the light.
— Ram Dass

Each day I will be reborn anew

Each Day I will be reborn anew
The dawn breaking with a golden hue
Writing the stories and pages of time
Creating poems with riddles and rhymes

Walking my soul down the paths gone before
Choosing a meaning of my story once more
Stretching the body and the mind
To do good deeds in whatever I find

Love and Laughter are mine to give
Joy and Peace are mine to live
God walks with me each step of the way
As I go along the path each day

All healing is essentially the release from fear. (ACIM, T-2.IV.1:7)

Everyday is new

Everyday is a new moment
a new opportunity for us to choose to be joyful and peaceful
Everyday has the power of now within
to let fear and guilt go
and know there is no sin

Everyday I find
and I know it starts with being kind
I know I will, I know I can
I know light and I understand

For each a moment which does give
my choice to determine how I live
for everyday can be given light
and love's unlimited might

Every thought is new
does it have value to you
and forgive those which do not last

No one would choose to let go what he believes has value. (ACIM,

T-15.VII.3:3)

Freedom

I held a bird fallen from the sky
I held it close, while it could not fly.
Soon the bird had begun to try
To spread its wings and reach for the sky

And one day it finally reached with all its might
Higher and higher it soared, until it was out of sight.
And I watched the sky until it was night
For her to come back within my sight

I look back and wonder what could have been,
If I had my little bird back again.

Gather and Nourish relationships

Gather and nourish relationships,
For they will pay dividends far greater than any material want
or need
And you will find your soul satisfied greater, and your needs
less,
And you strengthen those, who will also in turn strengthen you

Nourish and strengthen your relationship with God,
With your faith in whatever form it may be
Move towards it with confidence in your eternal self
Knowing that you are a creation of God and from God

With a definite purpose in his plan with your life
And eternal peace and joy of which spirit only knows
Nourish and strengthen your relationship with your spouse or
significant other
In them you will find a part of yourself

In them you will find two are stronger than one as they are one
Nourish and strengthen your relationship with your children
In them you see only unconditional love and find its true
meaning

In them is the world and you are their guide

For these 3 will build a foundation stronger than any
From here you can go onto a world of true meaning
Seeking truth, friendships, laughter, and love

As we work to create light for others, we naturally light our own way
— Mary Anne Radmacher

Gonna Break Away

Gonna Break Away
from the time today
thinking about what might have been
to a new blazing light within

no more excuses
no more holding back
the world is mine to make
and there is nothing I lack

so push on through
from that thought of pain
the sky is clearing
and there is no more rain

break away from that feeling
your mind is healing
and light shines deep inside
let it out, no need to hide

And now I see
I am forever free

let it out, let truth be
knowing the light is me

Let them all go, dancing in the wind, dipping and turning till they disappear from sight, far, far outside of you. [2]And turn you to the stately calm within, where in holy stillness dwells the living God you never left, and Who never left you. (ACIM, T-18.I.8:1-2)

Hidden pain and healing rain

We all have hidden pains
the times in our life we need the healing rain
when keep them within not knowing why
or how to let them go, no matter how hard we try

Some we know on the surface, many are under
as we move through the dark in pain of our slumber
But know there are many who are out there waiting for you
Many ways for the Healing rain to show you what is true

The Healing rain may be a friend within reach
Or a group you become part of with wisdom to teach
Or someone who goes with you and knows the pain you have
traveled
all can help pain unravel

and you too have a choice you can make
Others can help you find this
but this can be your journey to take
But know this, you are never alone

The Healing rain falls gently down

Washing away the pains
and it is with you today
many are with you each step

Their love is always with you
let them help and you will find this is true

Just as one candle lights another and can light thousands of other candles, so one heart illuminates another heart and can illuminate thousands of other hearts.
— Leo Tolstoy

How do you heal the world

Start with YOU
and know you are Love
within infinite Light
and One with your Creator

And you give Love to all
and understand many are calling for help – help them
and you know all are One with you – feel this
and you do not judge
all there is no past in anyone, including you

You have no enemies because we are all the same
You understand everyone is here for a reason
You are open minded
You Let things go

You see you don't really need to heal the world – you need to
heal yourself
and by doing so we will actually heal the world – because the
world is one with you

You give Love

You see Love in all
You forgive by overlooking
You focus on Now in time for that is all there is - the present

You are grateful
You are open minded
Leave to give - then give some more - that is what Love does

If you accept your function in the world of time as one of healing, you will emphasize only the aspect of time in which healing can occur. (ACIM, T-13.IV.9:2)

How high can you fly

Soaring, gliding, wings riding high
beyond the blue, sunlit sky
I reach for the stars as a busy world drifts by
not a care, do I dare, fleeting thoughts
as the wind whistling by

How high can you fly
do wings take flight
on a glorious sunlight night

Soaring above, a mind remembers
and our world of wings can take us there
with forgiveness and love we bring

For we travel to whence
we leave the past
a peace eternal, at Heaven at last

With each thought we make
we give and we take
but our wings give us sight
to love's eternal light

I will love the light for it shows me the way, yet I will endure the darkness because it shows me the stars.

— Og Mandino

I open the self

I open the self to the Holy Spirit
to let him guide the way
and guide the actions of today

I give to him the trust I will
to show through a seeming storm
the winds cease with "peace be still"

I give all thoughts away
hiding nothing from eternities sway
and into the world I laugh and play

I see with one what was two
I see the skies brilliant golden hue
no clouds cover the light
for I am within and all, his power and might

Go my child
release those pains
for in doing so
feel the healing rain

The Holy Spirit knows that you both have everything and are everything. (ACIM, T-4.III.9:5)

I will

The spirit, though not broken, is wounded
it searches for meaning on this celestial ball
something to hold onto, which will forever last
something which seems for me, to answer the call

A phoenix rising from the ashes
it will remain a brilliant light
it will rise again from these moments of pain
and take to the sky, in joyous flight

It knows no boundaries, though we may try
to limit and separate, to hide.
But deep inside I know what truly I am
an endless peace, and unlimited strength, in me abides

I am a reflection of what is within
with true reality of only pure love
forever to be with all my brothers
forever a spirit as pure as a snow white dove

Dark night, bright future
Like the phoenix from the ashes, I shall rise again

HEALING POEMS

-Dolly Parton

Don't forget the present moment

In all our busyness of the world, the cares, planning, and doing
Don't forget the present
For cares are fleeting and worry for naught
Don't bring them to the present
so it will know them not.

For past nor future, nor judgments bring not
for the light of day they surely will blot
Bring not things for they are not needed here
and time need not intrude on the present
the moment goes into eternity so clear

For Love only knows now
and love will always show you how
bring only this to your present
no judgments, toward you or others
let them fly away

Your present is a sacred place
and one which you can reach
close your eyes and you will find many thoughts
let them drift away one by one

until they fade away
replaced by only now
and the love you are and share
and your world will have no cares

*Everyone seen without the past thus brings you nearer to the end of
time by bringing healed and healing sight into the darkness, and
enabling the world to see.* [5] *(ACIM, T-13.VIII.5:4-5)*

Spread your love and light

Believe that you can
and you will begin to understand
you are an unlimited creator
of all the things a mind can dream
so go for that which you wish
spread you love and light all over the universe

Time to move on

Time to move on
Time to let go
The past is gone
and has nothing to show

Time to move beyond
worrying about future states
for spirit and love
are now your mate

It's time my friend
to make amends
to live in a moment
and find peace not torment

It's time to find
what is in your mind
time to be so bold
your story untold

It's time to let time depart
for really when did it start

you have power over all that it made
and can choose a much different way

So my friend be so very kind
through each perception of time
and know love is always within each
of the lessons I learn and am to teach

Love knows no time

To be born again is to let the past go, and look without condemnation upon the present. (ACIM, T-13.VI.3:5)

It just takes one

It just takes one
to let it all pass
it just takes one
to see it does not last

It just takes one
to feel love from all
it just takes one
to answer his call

it just takes one
to remember each time
it just takes one
to hear heaven's chime

It just take one thought
to remember what love has brought
what God has shared
what has been eternally sought

It just takes one
will it be you?

But choose the spirit, and all Heaven bends to touch your eyes and bless your holy sight, that you may see the world of flesh no more except to heal and comfort and to bless. (ACIM, T–31.VI.1:8)

It is time

It is time
to take action now
The Holy Spirit leads the way
to show you how

It is time
for love to be felt now
to extend it to all the world
it will always show you how

It is time
to let go of fear
to know its a thought mistaken
and not hold it dear

It is time
and in this moment I can
learn from this thought
and I will understand

It is time
for this little man

to know he has all power
beyond a 6 foot tower

And so we give
a thought of love
to the world we send
and peace and joy ascends

Look straight into the present

Look straight into the present
for that is what its for
looking neither forward or back
for they are but other doors

Look straight into the present
Now is here and all there will be
We travel through a space in time

Straight ahead!
Through fog and rain
Through time sublime
through any pains

Straight into the present
dive deep within its meaning
for you will find your peace
and no longer seek

*It doesn't take a lot of strength to hang on. It takes a lot of strength
to let go*
– J. C. Watts

New Beginnings

Here is to new beginnings
Each Breath in
revitalized and new
exhale and let it out
as we release our past

Each moment we choose
which one to hold on to
Each moment thoughts show
which joyful ones to let grow

Begin each day
Look in the mirror and say
I love you in a wonderful way
As it carries within the lights rays

Be kind to all
on this little ball
hold that deep within
for that is your call

and affirm that you

are worthy of all the love to
that God has given you
and all his creations too

And so with new beginnings
and love never ending
goes with you, for you, and is you
One with God, one will all

Each Day, each moment brings us a choice to make a new
beginning. Letting go of our past, of our guilt and realize the
beautiful spirit and the love that is within.

No matter

No matter where you have been
what you have or have not send
How much or little you have won or lost
How much you judge yourself worthy or not

No matter what was the score
No matter if the play was a bore
No matter if you have lost your way
No matter whatever you say

God loves you no matter what
and you should love yourself
without any question
and your brother goes with you
for all are worthy of his love
and no matter what
shining forever from above

No matter where you are
at this point in your life
You are love and are loved
through any pain or strife

You may feel off today
things may not have gone your way
but know you can remove all things
and let him carry them away

Close your eyes and look at those thoughts
one by one and what they have brought
then look with him as each one passes by
and let it go, for you know longer have to cry

and what is outside us all
is really within our minds
we need not change the world
but learn to ourselves be kind

No matter where you are
what is in the past or future
Love is here with you now
Let it in to show you how

*Never fear shadows. They simply mean there's a light shining
somewhere nearby*
— Ruth E. Renkel

Nothing can hurt me

Nothing can hurt me
No persons actions or deeds
I let them fly away and pay them no heed

The world will try
in so many, many ways
to take your peace of mind and hide your light
but whatever happens, you still shine eternally bright

Whatever action goes on anywhere
rather toward you or others know all seems to be there
and is a call for love or showing its way
the script goes on, don't let it take you away

Like a chapter in a book you can choose to turn the page
and listen to the love in your mind, and let it say
look beyond what perceptions will show
for indeed they are part of the stage we behold

*This is love: to fly toward a secret sky, to cause a hundred veils to
fall each moment. First to let go of life. Finally, to take a step
without feet.*

-Rumi

One thought can change your world

There is one thought which can change your world
One thought that brings instant joy forever
One Power to transcend time, space, or any place
One thought which brings truth to light shining forever bright

One which goes with us now and will show you how

That thought is Love
It can bring peace like a Dove
and needs no sacrifice
for to all it is so very nice

Love is here now, this very moment
One Thought can change your world – because it can change
your Mind

Do not underestimate the power of your mind
for it can create anything you wish
and extends love to all
extending beyond time and space

In one mind we all are joined

no matter what form
all are one

What we believe, we see
But, what is seen, may not be
as such, think about your true reality

What is known is yours to see
beyond a hidden veil
light is there for all eternity

As a child we sleep
with dreams so deep
with no forms we would keep
but show us a way
if only a little peep
and that is enough
for you to know
your true journey
and which way to go

Knowledge is Power because it is certain – A Course in Miracles

Our past and letting go

When we were children
many things may have happened
and we keep those memories for a long time
as we grow into adults

And some of those things may have appeared to be small
but we remember the pain they caused
and the same can be said for those big events in our lives
we remember those pains and carry them forward like clouds of
rain

Today is a new day and you can start letting go
of those past hurts and pains your life did show
You have grown stronger and wise
You can smile with a new day
and see a new sunrise

As the sun set let that hurt go
it no longer serves you
As when the sun has set let it go
for you and the event can now rest

You are loved no matter your past
You are perfect love
perfect light
forever

The key to change... is to let go of fear.
-Rosanne Cash

Outside and inside

What we see outside
is really inside
in, and out, and all about
up and down
things that make us frown
and then what can seems like miles
may indeed cause a smile
for we know not what is the cause
it seems to be outside which never does pause

And the good, and the bad
and all the silly things we had
change like the winds of our time
some with sounds and some not a rhyme

How can one become at peace with all
rather out or in, do we answer a call?
is it the cause or the effect?
Do I know what I see?
Or is it another reality?

So when you are distressed by what goes out there

Look within and see Love and Peace everywhere
Two becomes one when separate thoughts end
What message to yourself do you want to send?

*Do not dwell in the past, do not dream of the future, concentrate th
mind on the present moment. – Buddha*

Are you ready

Are you ready to get out there?
What questions remain
What is all different
Is really all the same

The mind holds the past
and the ego makes it last
as we swim on through our times
and all earthly rhymes

There are new people to meet
New things to learn and teach
New goals and friends to reach
New Love to give for all you greet

Are you ready to get out there?
And show the love you have to share
and give it all, without a care
Light from within not somewhere out there!

Are you ready to look outside
and know all the love we see with eyes

is sometimes hidden deep inside
Are you ready?
Yes you are

Light and shadow are opposite sides of the same coin. We can illuminate our paths or darken our way. It is a matter of choice.
–Maya Angelou

I let go

Letting go, setting free
what was then, and what is to be
Love goes on, perhaps in thought alone
a setting sun, a new horizons home

It matters not who let it go first
or who held on the longest to quench the thirst
it knows no boundaries though we make a lot
it shares unending here or not

So great it rights the many wrongs
taking its place to always belong
showing the way in joy or pain

When I let go, falling into the air
floating, falling without a care
become one with all around
nothing holding, free unbound

In time set free of all world realities
in a place not seen by any face
for I need not let go after all

I need but change a mind about the fall

When I let go of what I am, I become what I might be.
–Lao Tzu

Sail on

The fish are plenty and the ports are many
Sail on to the destinations with joy
with love for the many faces
and grateful for the many places

Knowing your brothers and sisters are always with you
journeying on this one trip
across the deep blue sea
aboard our celestial spiritual ship

We go as one
perhaps seen as two
We understand now
that all travel together with you

And the love we share
is always there
no matter the form
no matter when we are born

So sail on my friend
feel the joy and not the pain

The Light is always shining
through any thunder and rain

The Holy Spirit uses special relationships, which you have chosen
support the ego, as learning experiences that point to truth. Und
*His teaching, **every relationship becomes a lesson in love.** – A*
Course in Miracles

Seek and find

Searching in a world
for that peace and joy within
takes us far and wide on a journey
which we know not, where it began

Answers are but fleeting
for soon we seek for more
in a world so full of questions
and we move through another door

Seeking for salvation
searching for our home
knowing not the question
is this where we belong?

Once we did remember
a fleeting thought not new
and that light within is his answer
to the world which is true

So my brother seek within the mind
for it is only here that you will find

the question to the answers
is only one, loving, joyous, and kind

*It's so much darker when a light goes out than it would have been
it had never shone.*
— John Steinbeck

The flower

The flower was planted at a young age
from the seed spouted
the leaves grew as we do in our lives
shaping the plant – growing to new heights

And we water and nourish the tender plant
and as she grew we provided more soil
and the roots moved deeper

And one day I noticed the small pods appear
for the plant was ready to blossom my dear
and the next day a beautiful flower of red and gold appeared
it was the most beautiful site to behold

and soon more flowers we began to see
and we continued to water and nurture the plant
each day

and one day we noticed a few leaves turning brown
and flowers began to wilt which brought us a frown
and as the leaves turned brittle we decided to trim them off
and soon the flower raised their heads again to the glory of the

sun

And so in life we plant the seeds which are sown
and water and nourish the things we have known
and we all raise each day to a glorious day
and give our gifts of love to the world this way

some times we must trim our leaves from the past
they have given their all but our growth requires they fall
and so they slip away and we reform a new
for by letting go we are now stronger and renewed

Only in the darkness can you see the stars.
-Martin Luther King Jr.

The flute of forgiveness

Play on, the flute of forgiveness
whenever the world rushes on
and takes our mind away
and anger seems to be your day
play on your flute
and whisk those clouds away

and when your peace of mind
has take a turn to the unkind
play a note on your flute so high
and watch those thoughts go on by

forgive is merely to remember only the loving thoughts you gave
the past, and those that were given you. – A Course in Miracles

The Healing rain

The healing rain, falls gently down
Washing away the past, with such a soothing sound
Cleansing us whole, as it bathes the earth
the spirit reborn, refreshed, a new celestial birth

The clouds though gray at this moment in time
will soon give way to a sun which shines
and a sky which is brilliant blue
makes our spirits soar as we remember what is true

Each drop which falls has a rainbow within
for each has the power to create and begin
water takes shape in endless forms
as it travels a path forever reborn

and like the spirit which knows no end
for it came to life before time began
and travels a path known only to one
for it seeks for a time and then is done

soon the sun will rise again with a brilliant shine
our spirits soar as we remember what Love is all mine

and the rain has washed any sins past
for a light in you shines forever it will last

*Healing rain is a real touch from God. It could be physical healing
or emotional or whatever.*
  –Micheal W. Smith

The hole in my heart

There once was a hole in my heart
left by someone where my love was a part
love thought to be so whole I saw
but feelings after left me feeling so raw

I have learned through years gone by
the hole I thought was there no longer abides
for my heart has always been whole

What emptiness felt which love showed I had
was really something deeper
showing me a way to heal

For I know now I have always been whole
what in within eternally shines so bright
and when someone goes away
and our eyes no longer meet or bodies sway
does not mean they take away part of our heart
for it is whole and complete

we know its not easy for us to do
but just think on these thoughts

and understand the real you

And be grateful for the one who showed to you
the hole you thought was there
and the love between the two
For the hole you thought was there
was a thought of something missing out there
but indeed inside you are not missing anything
all the love you need you already have
You are whole, you are love
You are light, and you are joy

You have always been a whole heart
and this is your new start

No situation is so dark that there is not a ray of light!
— Norman Vincent Peale

The Little voice

There is a little voice inside.
It speaks to me day or night
it speaks of a brilliant light
it speaks of truth
an unending might

There is another voice which speaks
anger, hurt, worldly cares
blame, guilt, and sin

Which voice will you listen to today
Which seed will you grow further along the way
The little voice speaks of light and love
grow it into a mighty oak which reaches into heaven above

For from a tiny seed is sown salvation's path
from a tiny seed faith grows forever to last
from a tiny seed peace shall be
it starts small like the mustard seed

Like a grain of sand washed upon the shore
our faith grows more and more

resting in love and opening all doors
leaving a past we do not let it last

Listen today to love's warm embrace
listen to your heart's song
and grow the seed, the little voice
of hope, and joy for light is your choice

You were created in Love like itself
the Love of God, your love eternal
Join in him now, grow the seed
for he will show you how
the little voice, is all you need

Keep your face always toward the sunshine, and shadows will fall behind you.
— Walt Whitman

the Looking glass

The looking glass
What image is me.
is something that I love
What do I see?

The mirror is foggy at mornings light
as we wipe away the sleep of the night
and what begins to come into view
a symbol of love in its colorful hues

The looking glass show all our cares
but really do we see them up in the air?
What eyes will show surely does not contain
that which is within the heavenly domain

It is but a symbol to be thought with love
A symbol of beauty from heaven above
What do you see looking back at thee
For you are Love, and always will be

You are a mirror of truth, in which God Himself shines in perfe
light. (ACIM, T-4.IV.9:1)

The Power is you

The Power is you
given by the infinite to be that which you choose
to be in all thought, actions, and deeds
to be the best in all you do
to climb the mountains
and see the wonder of the view
to transcend the mind, to transcend time
to reach all of your brothers and love one another

To feel joy in every moment
to be at peace, to learn, and teach
Realize the unlimited you is all you have to do
for you have the power to choose
which makes all power given, to you.

A candle loses nothing when it lights another candle.
— Thomas Jefferson

The precious present

The precious present is here to last
the trick is letting a mind move on from the past.
for we dwell on things which seem good or bad
and either way we are stuck on what we had

And its not that feeling this way means we are lost
but it is understanding that it does have a cost
for the precious present seems to be hard to find
and we search externally for it within our mind

And it is always there like the chapter of a book
we choose what we wish so we do not have to look
at the eternal present where peace and love reside
and no thought we bring from our past that it hides

So whatever the form you bring with you now
which your path has taken you on somehow
release it into the air and let it go
for the present is here for you to now hold

And extend the present to all with your love
and join with them within the light of heaven above

As one now free from the dreams and from all
for you have made the choice of the present's call

esterday is gone. Tomorrow has not yet come. We have only today.
et us begin.

— Mother Theresa

The spirit I am

And now the time has come for me to be
a true spirit that you can no longer see
but I will be in your heart and mind
I will be there in everything so kind

I will be the wind behind your back
I will be the sea, rolling on an endless track
I will be the sunlight warming your face
I will be rain, watering the earth to create a beautiful place

All that is beauty is all that I will be
All thoughts within you of goodness I will see
All things upon the planet will my joy will share
All our love we share with you, with no more cares

For in spirit we are one and always will be
In spirit is love, an everlasting moment
In spirit is peace for all of life's rhymes
In spirit we are heaven sent

Take a moment each day
to let your spirit fly away

and join with mine in wherever you rest
Remember I am with you and forever will be

And behold, I am with you always, to the end of the age.
Jesus – Matthew 28:20

Be Kind

Be kind to yourself
by being kind to others
Be grateful for all
and for each sister and brother

Forgive thoughts and things
which joy does not bring
see the light within
let healing begin

To tinker or tickle

Tinker or to tickle
is the world a big jar of pickles?
Rising up before our eyes
like the dawn of a new sunrise

we tinker with all within the race
running fast with no end in place
we play with toys we seem to find
all within the realm of the mind

and by and by we learn to laugh
a tickle a day our little bath
a thought now not quite so seriously
moving towards being fearlessly

So when you find you have a choice
choose to tickle not tinker within that voice

Laughter is the sun that drives winter from the human face.
-Victor Hugo

Today is my day of release

Today is a new day
Yesterday is gone
and with all from our past
is just part of a light, happy song

We all are brand new
with a new start to it all
No thought, no word, or deed
do we hold onto on this little ball

All power we have at every moment
for we have the choice within the mind
to seek for love, joy, and happiness
or whatever we wish to find

And that is the choice we all must make
what do you seek and why do we
for in that question the purpose will arise
and within the light we learn to see

When you feel those thoughts arise
Lay them down at he Holy Spirits feet of truth

to be removed forever from my mind
and illusion you will no longer find

and let those thoughts go to him who knows the way
and at this moment, start a brand new day

*he past is nothing. [9]Do not seek to lay the blame for deprivation
n it, for the past is gone. [10]You cannot really not let go what has
lready gone (ACIM, T-16.VII.2:8-10)*

Let it go

Let it go
off into the wind
for the joy it was
or the pain the has been

Let it go
off in a distance
a spark still shines through
for all is now and new

Let it go for holding onto things
does not bring everlasting joy
within the song it sings

Let it go
a past is no longer
a day, a week, a year or more
by letting them go, you will be stronger

It's being here now that's important. There's no past and there's no
future. Time is a very misleading thing. All there is ever, is the now.
We can gain experience from the past, but we can't relive it; and we

n hope for the future, but we don't know if there is one."
— George Harrison

I'm at peace with the world

I am at peace with the world
I am at peace with me
I am at peace with the divine
and all that is to be

I am at peace now
as my source will show me how
as I open my mind
and release what he finds

I am at peace now I let go
all thoughts, judgments, beliefs
things of the world
I now do not seek

and a deep peace descends
on me and I understand
all thoughts are one
and in light peace has no end

For the Present is the point at which time touches eternity.
— **C.S. Lewis**

The change

We all seek change upon this home
a vast ocean searching endlessly, alone
to find our lost peace, our lack, our love
we forget peace lies in heaven above

for what little things are found below
with the to and fro the bodies do show
with legions of choices here to make
which is real, the truth? which is fake?

Rolling through seemingly treacherous times
meaning found not, perhaps some sublime
asking questions for answers not meant to be
that we rests in love's eternity

but a gift was given to us one and all
a gift of light which answers every call
The answer to all is the spark lit within
and remembering each thought can mend

My brother seek no more in this place
for time and space are a mistaken race

Look beyond these eyes and find
a loving and peaceful, change of mind

*Don't wait for the world to change. Change your mind about the
world.*
— **Alan Cohen**

The Quiet Center

There is a place within which we can reach
There is a place inside which we teach
a quiet center we seek to understand
calm within this little man

a place were all are thought of as equals
a time of rest from the bodies sequels
knowing who goes with us, hand in hand
knowing we chose peace wherever we can

God knows us in this quiet place
for we stop and remember we are not in the race
and guilt is no more
for forgiveness has left it at heaven's door

the world still may scream and shout
and try to divert thoughts to what it is about
but within the center knowledge shows its might
and we enter into, the quiet of the light

et there will always be this place of rest to which you can return.

And you will be more aware of this quiet center of the storm tha
all its raging activity. This quiet center, in which you do nothing
will remain with you, giving you rest in the mist of every busy doir
on which you are sent.
– A Course in Miracles Chapter 18 –7 v 8

Know or no

There are no limits, you only place them on yourself
here are no emotions, but joy, all others are a mistaken choice
so what have we learned and what would you choose?

No pain in your true state of grace
No sorrow do not dwell in that place
No choices but one in each circumstance
Know that there really is nothing by chance

Know that you are love
feel it each moment
and know your brothers too
for behind them all, is you

Know peace
no anger
Know Love
no strangers

Know joy
no sorry
Know you

and be at Peace at last

We know what we are, but know not what we may be.
-William Shakespeare

Within the Ocean of Love

All fears dissolve wash away those worries
in the Ocean of God's love and forgiveness
the sands may wash upon the shore
and his love removes them from our minds core

Our pain, our loses, our anger, our lack of peace
will ebb and flow throughout of lives
and when they come to mind and the hurt you feel
Let them go, and wash into the ocean of love

a grain of sorry, a pebble of fear
wash away in the love that is here
hurts rather near or far, past or present
wash away in love's ocean becoming your present

Within God's love, all the little grains of sin, guilt, and fear are
washed way
they are let go and off into the tides, his love sweeps them away
dissolved by the waves of love which rush in
leaving us whole within his light we understand we are
eternally bright

No matter the pain as we walk on the shores
a Heavenly rain washes them away
and into his ocean they disappear for all time
The Ocean of Love knows no limits
for what it can heal you of today

Things which wash up and wash away
Wood, rocks, all types of "things
God's love keeps the waves coming
and gently what we carry is gone forever

The rivers of our lives
bring all to him
and we heal in love
and we feel the heavenly hue

whatever the dunes
whatever the tune
let it go into the ocean
of a heavenly potion

and when that ship
is at rest upon the shores
let him meld it in love
to be seen no more

and our bodies may enter
with whatever the pains
and the waters will wash away
whatever hurts us today

and the stones and rocks there
will one day dissolve with into his care
and the ocean gently washing slowly away
and the light shines upon the new day

*There is always light. If only we're brave enough to see it. If only
we're brave enough to be it.* – Amanda Gorman

·

What are those thoughts

What are those thoughts lingering on
Some hidden some not
perhaps just a brief spot
in the past hide but today live
what lesson is this trying to give

reaching far reaching close
time has no meaning for which they boast
but we keep them alive perhaps with pain
is there really anything for us to gain?

step inside, look within
look at each thought forgive with him
for ideas leave not their source as they say
so forgive those old thoughts this very day

Let them go into the whispering winds
Let them be replaced by the love he sends

People like us, who believe in physics, know that the distinction between past, present, and future is only a stubbornly persistent illusion.

— **Albert Einstein**

What is the problem

What is the problem?
They seem so varied
Like a deep ocean sea
they rise and fall, appear to be

One is resolved
or so we think
another then falls
and then we sink

Behind the veil
Of what seem manipulation
is one thought withheld
of all our tribulations

Separate from our source
we think we stand
apart, wondering
on a desolate land

But into eternity we are joined
with our God, or brothers

all thoughts of love
one which cannot be undone

So as we travel the road each day
remember the answer given
to each seeming problem
which arises and say

God is one
and I am with God
Forever lighting a path
rather here or far

You are invulnerable

There is nothing to fear
for nothing attacks love my dear
thoughts that swirl in the mind
look for a target a body to find

But remember you are infinite love
and thoughts do not harm
if you fear attack
you believe

Live your life
No Fear
No Limits
No Excuses!

Above all else I want to see
Love and Light
in all take flight
Time and Space
is no longer a race
All are one

hero is an ordinary individual who finds the strength to persevere and endure in spite of overwhelming obstacles.

–Christopher Reeve

Your worth

What is your worth?
Can you find it on earth?
What is really at your core
What is behind the hidden door?

We seek our worth outside to define
what is within and love to find
trying and endless maze of pursuits
wearing many hats and fancy suits

but they all point to just one thing
seek ye not outside for it will be in vain
for is found within does not take form
Love is always and will so remain

So what do we have to judge our worth?
but the knowledge that God created you perfect
, eternal, love, and light, extending forever far beyond any
universe
and that is all we remember when
with one we extend with him
and we never begin, and never end

Straight into the present

Look straight into the present
nor forward or back
the past floats on by
like a cloud high in the sky

The future, the past
no to be found, they won't last
a home to build and seek and find
love is found, only in the mind

and one with God, for we all share
our earthly goals, spirit has no cares
a wisp of wind

Look straight in the present
for that is where love is found

Straight into the present
Is God's gift to you
One with his love
one in heaven above

For you seek not in idols
past nor tomorrow
for only in those
will you find more sorrow

Focus on his present to you
It is now, it is here
and eternally shared with all
Love will always be his call

I have realized that the past and future are real illusions, that the
exist in the present, which is what there is and all there is.
-Alan Watts

Live in the now

Live in the moment
your mind is only now
focus each thought on your present
and peace will show you how

For tomorrow will be
and yesterday shows no more
Now is your time
to open the love of Heaven's door

Now does not depend
on what has been
You have the power now
to choose again

ew of us ever live in the present. We are forever anticipating what
is to come or remembering what has gone.
— Louis L'Amour

Rest if you may

Rest my friend if you may
from the labors of yesterday
Rest from all that seem to burden you mind
and deep within peace you will find

Rest another moment in time
in a world of riddles and of rhymes
Pause and sink into the infinity of now
time is yours and with him will show you how

Pause and feel your thoughts release
and drift off into a twilight
the sun will rest another day
then rise in glorious dawning light

And that dawning will be you
shining upon all things fresh and new
as your light

Make the best use of what is in your power, and take the rest as
happens.
- Epictetus

When the world gets you down

When the world gets you down
and you want to smile but you have a frown
Know that all we see in this world of oops
is really just a bowl of silly soup!

Learn to laugh at the little things
Learn to see the light and joy you bring
And whenever you can, help a brother
for we go hand in hand with one another

Life will test us this we know
we so many things or eyes do show
But remember whether they seem good or bad
the Silly Soup will gently smile inside your head

So take those thoughts of sin, guilt and fear
or depression, anxiety, inadequacy, or tears
Let them all blend into a silly soup bowl
and in gentle laughter, let them all go!

For we all swim together in a group
Laughing in giant bowl of garlic soup

Oh we splash and may play for awhile
but we gently move on into the light, and smile

The greatest healing therapy is friendship and love.
–Hubert H. Humphrey

Thoughts on comparing and judging

We do not measure up in something, rather career,
ationships, finances, fitness, our looks, or status is life, how
ve communicate. The list is endless because our belief in a
ody and those things which we let impact us in our lives in
ndless. Being a body means we limit ourselves in our mind
d when we do this of course we will not measure up to others,
r we may feel we are greater than they are. Whether we feel
:le or great to our ego it does matter. We attached our minds
to the "body" and our journey is on.

e judge the body and our place within it and project outside
hat we wish which hurts or makes it feel wonderful. It does
atter which for from this perspective the ego wins and keeps
ır mind preoccupied with a little spec of dust when we a far,
r, greater than this. We are in fact one with God, our source
and infinite Love and Joy. Why would God have any limits,
ich most of us do believe, but we don't believe we have limits
for we don't believe we are one with him.

One thought

One thought can heal it all
Just one thought on this little ball
it is time to answer its call
and share within to extend

A thought of one, Love it can
begin to heal and understand
his and ours, we command
A thought with such power for all to mend

The mighty, the gentle, the light within
the kindness, embracing, message it sends
the answer to all things upon a world depends
is the thought of love, let us begin

*Think and extend love, light, and peace to those you meet, those
you think about, those you teach. Whether in the past, present, or
future, all times are the same and all healing is done with one
thought.* – Mark Helm from "You are Light"

Believe you can

Believe you can
and seek to understand
the world takes form
and into it we are born

Belief makes reality
and we search for our senility
in all we do, think, and say
thoughts have all power to sway

Believe you are one with God and all
and every form on this little ball
Traveling down many paths
and let him lead you through the mountain pass

Believe you have unlimited joy within
and you certainly have no sin
and guilt is gone disappearing in the wind
and we let go of all we think we have been

Yes my friend you can do whatever you wish
Life is about remembering your eternal heavenly bliss!

and share that thought for all to see
for you and I just have to be

Healing is a matter of time, but it is sometimes also a matter of
opportunity.
-Hippocrates

About the Author

Also by Mark Helm

My passion is to help you on your journey to find the love ar
light within. There are many paths we do this by and many wa
we learn each day. My books and poems may spark somethin
within you to help you or someone else.

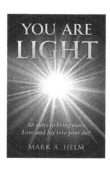

You Are Light
Look at your challenges in a new light, ar
look at all other people in a new way sin
they share their light with you and you w
see your light as well. Find more light ea
day and increase your Love and Joy ste
by step as we climb higher and higher ar
understand the truth of who we are.

YOU ARE LIGHT: 88 ways to bring more Love and Joy into your d
is a guide that helps you learn how to see and feel the light fro
many different perspectives. Learn to uncover the darkne
within by shining a little light each day to help you find you
way.

Do you feel like You Are Light? Our world can show us unlimite
barriers to finding the light within and we feel the darkne
surround us in so many ways. We limit ourselves, we lim
others, and judge all things all the time. We seek light but ar
not sure where to look. We look at a world of chaos and try t
make sense of what is going on, what its purpose is, and wha
my purpose is. Where is the Light?

One in Love and Light

One in Love and Light are poems which speak to the love and light within you and all others for we all go as one in spirit, one with our source and creator, reminding us whatever we see before our eyes, we know eternal peace and joy are what we truly share within. As we rise each day, Love and Light will help u find your way and bring a smile to your soul for this is hoice you can behold. Remember, the light always shines yond the clouds we travel through. We always have a choice choose again for how we feel inside, and you my friend, will ht the way for others by doing so.

Dreams

Dreams – Poems of Dreaming in the Night and Awakening to the light are a collection of poems to help you realize the light is within you and all others no matter what darkness we move through. Let go of fear, anger, guilt, and lack of peace and know your light transcends them all and spark your mind to k at our lives in a new perspective and the events which go in our world and within our minds.

ny of these poems I wrote when I was writing my book "You Light" after going through some of those challenging years self and I hope to help you on your journey to see the light d love not only within you but all your brothers and sisters.

PEACE MATTERS
thoughts to bring Peace within

MARK A HELM

Peace Matters

Mark has written some ideas to help y
become more peaceful each day, ea
moment. The first step is to recognize y
are not at peace which we easily do, the 2
step is understanding you have a choice
maintain your peace or not. The power
your mind is all yours in every instance.

Milton Keynes UK
Ingram Content Group UK Ltd.
UKHW020250221123
432980UK00016B/850